Praise for Sherri Elliott-Yeary, Bestselling Author

"In the not for profit organizational space, failure to understand, harness and accept the power of generational differences is the difference between mission success or failure. Sherri's insights are insightful and invaluable."

Paul A. Markowski, CAE
Chief Executive Officer
American Association of Clinical Endocrinologists

"*Crack the Millennial Code* provides thought-provoking realities you need to consider. It affords actionable ideas on how to gain better understanding of what drives today's workforce and marketplace to deliver exceptional results."

George Killebrew
SVP of Corporate Sponsorship
Dallas Mavericks

"I believe this is the most challenging time in our history, particularly in business, for understanding, relating to, blending and working with the different generations. Sherri Elliott-Yeary's new series: *Crack the Millennial Code* is a masterful work that not only gives an understanding of generational differences, but also how to engage effectively with Millennials. I highly recommend *Crack the Millennial Code* to anyone in business to utilize Sherri's blueprint for generational success."

Gary Barnes
President
GaryBarnesInternational.com

"I remember clearly the day I offered to pick up my niece at the airport. I told her just to call me when the plane landed. She hesitated and then asked, 'Can I just text you?' I realized she hesitated because she wasn't sure I knew how to text message and didn't want to be rude if I didn't (I did). I had to smile, though, because this intergenerational exchange was just a microcosm of what's going on in workplaces every day. Sherri Elliott-Yeary provides helpful insights into the nature of and reasons for these generational differences and offers strategies for leveraging them to an organization's advantage."

Susan R. Meisinger, SPHR
Past President
Society for Human Resource Management

"If you want results, the most important thing that any of us can   do in today's ever-changing world is to truly understand the needs of the human beings we're hoping to lead or influence without judgment. Sherri's new *Crack the Millennial Code* series is an excellent resource to help any business gain a foundational understanding of the core needs for the 'largest generation in American History."

Kimberly Davis
Author of Brave Leadership: *Unleash Your Most Confident, Powerful, and Authentic Self to Get the Results You Need*

"If you think this book is another research book—think again. **Crack the Millennial Code** offers a direct line into the lives of this generation and explains what drives their behavior. This series isn't just for "marketers" who want to reach people, but in fact anyone who works or lives with Millennials and strives to connect with a new audience, or simply wants to understand the new world of engagement that we live in today."

Dr. Alise Cortez
Engagement Coach

Crack the Millennial Code:

Strategies to Manage Millennials

Sherri Elliott-Yeary, SPHR

Best Selling Author of Ties to Tattoos:
Turning Generational Differences into a Competitive Advantage

Published by Generational Guru
An Imprint of Soar 2 Success Publishing
Soar2SuccessPublishing.com

ISBN: 9781949087017
Printed in the USA

Cover Design by Chris Mendoza
ChrisdMendoza.com
Back Cover and Interior Headshot by Vanessa Corral Photography
VanessaCorral.com

Bulk discounts available.
For details visit *GenerationalGuru.com* or contact Sherri Elliott-Yeary at
469-971-3663 or *Sherri@GenerationalGuru.com*

Dedication

"When you are finished changing, you're finished."

Benjamin Franklin

This book is dedicated to the amazing Millennials in my life. They encourage me to be open to change and to think outside of the box.

I am also grateful to my granddaughter Aubrey who reminds her Grams that life is meant to be FUN and I should never forget to play like I am a child from time to time!

Thank you to my husband Manny for encouraging me to take on this important and timely project.

Most of all, thank you to my readers who support and encourage me to continue writing on the importance of generational diversity and inclusion.

Table of Contents

How to Read This Book .... Page 5

Introduction .... Page 7
We Are All Managers of Millennials

Chapter One .... Page 11
Understanding Millennials

Chapter Two .... Page 15
Millennials in the Workplace

Chapter Three .... Page 25
Attracting Top Millennial Talent

Chapter Four .... Page 35
The Millennial Mindset and Work Ethic

Chapter Five .... Page 49
Transparency, Feedback, and Leadership

Chapter Six .... Page 61
Lead the Way: Bridging the Gap Between the Generations

Conclusion .... Page 74

What's Next .... Page 77

Notes .... Page 79

About the Author .... Page 85

Preface

While many of my friends were partying and enjoying their college experience, I was busy taking with a full class load, working full time, and running both our catering and restaurant businesses. Those were not easy years, but I can honestly say those were great years.

Through the difficult times, I got to where I am now. I largely attribute this success to my unwavering persistence and resilience.

Today, I am the proud owner of a growing consulting practice and a motivational speaker for my training business, The Generational Guru. I work with, lead, and mentor Millennials.

Many believe that Millennials are lazy, entitled, unmotivated and have no loyalty to their company. However, I have found Millennials to be hard-working, dedicated, innovative and engaged. The secret to my work and success today is largely due to **#MillennialsMatter**.

As I worked with clients, and we invested time and energy into training and developing their Millennial employees, not only did their skills improve but quite interestingly I learned something unique from every Millennial.

With their domination of the workforce, the Millennial Generation has become the most scrutinized generation of all time. You can't attend a conference, scroll through a news feed, or watch a movie without seeing the mention of Millennials.

Millennials are heavily scrutinized because...

- They are the largest generation on the planet.

- They make up most of the labor force.

- They approach work much differently than previous generations.

- They have different buying habits.

- They represent future change and potential disruption.

- They have skills and knowledge that previous generations don't possess.

- They have begun to step into decision-making roles.

- They have been largely misunderstood and mislabeled.

- They have unrealistic expectations of what working for a living means; it's not just for a PAYCHECK.

Because Millennials are so highly scrutinized, it's likely that you have some understanding of who Millennials are, and the challenges they bring into the workplace.

Crack the Millennial Code: Strategies to Manage Millennials will build on that knowledge (or clear-up any misconceptions) to provide you with a clear, fresh, and forward-thinking understanding of Millennials. **You then will be equipped with proven strategies that will enable you to increase productivity, improve retention, and accelerate the development of your Millennial workforce.**

Over the years of speaking to thousands of people who manage Millennials, I've learned first-hand the specific challenges they face. These challenges have become more and more urgent, so I decided to create this book series to provide leaders a manual for effectively managing, developing, and engaging Millennials at work.

In this book, I share the results of all my research. I also share the reasoning and arguments behind each of these tips. This is done with the hope you can immediately implement the methodologies that you want in your own team, as well as understand why you want to use them and why they work. Understanding the rationale, you will be able to customize or personalize any of these techniques to fit your organization in the way that you feel will work best.

Should you have additional questions after finishing this book, please contact me via my website: *generationalguru.com* or *crackthemillennialcode.com* There you will also find resources, eBooks and guides that can assist you in your journey to creating a highly motivated and engaged generational workforce.

How to Read This Book

As the title suggests, this book is a manual to assist you in **Cracking the Millennial Code.** It's filled with instructions to help you learn specifically about Millennials. The book is meant as a quick reference guide for solving (nearly) all the challenge's leaders face when managing Millennials. Hint: Keep it handy.

You don't have to read this book straight through, but if you do, you'll be a master of Millennials. However, each chapter stands alone, so you can jump between them and choose the ones that are most useful to you and use the book as your personal map for leading, developing, and engaging Millennials.

(Note: I highly recommend that you read the "Generations Overview" section (pages 8-10) through first to get a foundation and useful context for the rest of the book and then read the chapters that are most pertinent for you.)

Happy reading and leading!

Sherri

Introduction

We Are All Managers of Millennials

"We now have a responsibility... to help this amazing, idealistic, fantastic generation [Millennials] build their confidence, learn patience, learn social skills, and find a better balance between life and technology – because quite frankly, it's the right thing to do." - Simon Sinek

We all "**manage**." We manage our finances, our household, our projects, our business, our peers, our family, our health, our hobbies, and every other aspect of life. Within each realm, a variety of challenges exist, with one of the biggest being the diversity of people with whom we are required to interact.

Not only are people diverse, but so are their expectations, level of engagement, abilities, goals, sensitivities, work ethic, backgrounds, beliefs, family structure, priorities, and more. Many if not most of these differences can be grouped into generational differences, and when we don't understand the dynamics in play, chaos ensues, and no one wins.

The challenges caused by Generational Diversity are not going away anytime soon. In fact, they will only increase as today's Millennial generation has graduated from college and they try to find their place in society, both personally and professionally.

This book is part two of my three-part series – **Crack the Millennial Code: How to *Market to, Manage & Motivate Millennials.*** Each book was created to provide you with greater insights into what Generational Diversity is and how it impacts your relationships, social interactions, and businesses.

Today, more than ever, finding productive ways to work across the generational divide is critical, and those who do this well will have a significant generational advantage over those who don't.

Identifying generational distinctions can provide a useful framework for building awareness and understanding of the different viewpoints, attitudes, needs, and experiences among generations, as well as the future changes in the workplace. Understanding these unique generational differences can become a competitive advantage for organizations in terms of higher productivity and increased employee engagement.

This is especially important for those looking to recruit Millennials for positions that require interaction and teamwork with coworkers, customers, and authority figures from different generations.

Generations Overview

Traditionalists - Born 1944 and Before

- Grew up in a manufacturing era where physical labor and assembly line work was more common and rewarded than knowledge capital.

- Prefer personal contact and connection, or a live person versus a telephone call or email.

- Tend to be wary of new technology and may find it intimating and confusing to learn, e.g., ATM's, voice mail, etc.

Baby Boomers - Born 1945 to 1964

- The rise of television transformed social habits.

- Were in the forefront of creating digital revolutions; 1970s technological revolution was beginning to replace manufacturing as the core of the economy.

- Technology is important to the current lifestyle at work and home but is a challenge to learn.

Generation X - Born 1965 to 1979

- Technology literate - the first generation to grow up with VCR's, personal PC's, video games, and MTV.

- Grew up in an environment of instant information, such as open investigative reporting on TV and access to any type of information via the Internet.

- More educated than previous generations.

Millennials – Born 1980 to 1996

- Grew up surrounded by digital media and are more confident, knowledgeable, and device-literate than prior generations.

- Use of technology has created demands for instant gratification.

- Customize their digital world as new products come onto the market.

- Extensive on-line users and can locate information easily and instantly on the Internet and through social networking.

Generation Z – Born 1997 and Later

- They are cynical and tend to be more realistic.

- They are private when sharing on social media.

- They are entrepreneurial. They want to be pioneers, not merely settle for a career.

- They are multi-taskers, preferring to work on five screens at a time.

- They are hyper-aware of their surroundings at work and home.

- They are technology reliant. They put technology in same category as air and water.

For a more extensive review, please purchase a copy of the first book in this series – **Crack the Millennial Code: Strategies to Market to Millennials** or visit **GenerationalGuru.com/Generations**.

Chapter One

Understanding Millennials

Before we begin to dissect the mental DNA of a Millennial, it's only fitting that we define who a Millennial is. The Millennial generation was born 1980 to 1996. "Millennial" was coined simply because they were being born just before the turn of the millennium. This generation is also less commonly referred to as "Generation Why"—a continuation of the receding "Generation X"—and has a negative tone like "Gen Why, Why, Why?" etc.

Millennials are the largest segment of workers in the U.S. workforce, fast approaching the 50% mark. Like it or not, it is highly probable that half of your organization's revenue or lack of it will be directly related to your Millennial employees. Statisticians say, at a minimum, 50 percent of the applicants you get at your organization are from Millennials. By 2025, Millennials will represent 75% of the U.S. workforce. To stay successful, organizations, leaders, managers and entrepreneurs must learn how to understand, embrace, and effectively manage and motivate Millennials.

Most of the leaders, recruiters and/or HR representatives I speak with have little to no expertise working with Millennials and they remain nervous about hiring them into their organization. Because of all the negative behaviors and traits they have heard about Millennials, some managers go to great lengths to avoid hiring them. This *"fear of the unknown"* plagues many who could benefit from a more open mind.

If we analyze the way this generation thinks and acts, we can capitalize on their sheer abundance and utilize their unique strengths to boost our organizations, which is just what I have helped many of my clients do.

Growing Up as A Millennial

For us to understand why Millennials act and think the way they do, we need to understand what growing up was like for Millennials.

Do you remember what "world experience" dominated child-rearing theology as they were growing up? **Participation Was Enough.**

Millennials as kids were put in sports teams and extracurricular activities by their parents so they could develop new skills and abilities. Sounds like the rest of the generations, right? Yes, except for one very different variable.

During these years, a huge shift occurred. Everyone suddenly worked to protect a child's self-value. The media advised young parents: "A child with low self-value is more likely to have suicidal thoughts later in life." Of course, this is enough to traumatize any parent.

A domino effect followed, until teachers and coaches felt the same pressure to avoid any actions that could possibly lower a child's self-value. At the end of the football season, everyone on the team suddenly had to receive an award. Coaches and teachers weren't truly able to recognize the "superstar performers." Instead, they were required to come up with creative ways to acknowledge every single kid on the team for something, simply to ensure they all received an equal award and their self-value was intact.

This may have made complete sense to parents, but they were robbing their children of one of life's most valuable lessons: ***there are always winners and losers***. If you truly want to be great, you need to out-work the loser.

Millennials were unfortunately conditioned that all they had to do was show up and participate to be rewarded.

In previous generations, there had always been clear winners and losers. You would get a reward or pay increase only when you excelled, and you would get a poor review if your performance was subpar. But Millennials have never had that experience.

Parents began challenging the authority of teachers and their grading, writing complaint letters to college deans for not accepting their child into their college, confronted hiring managers who did not choose their adult child for an internship, and went to U.S. Military Recruiting offices to inform sergeants how to properly care for and speak to their Millennial adult child.

Many Millennials have not been taught how to cope with disappointment, how to handle their own challenges, or how to push through difficult circumstances that are meant to stretch and grow them into productive, proactive adults.

In summary, they haven't learned: **"If you want to be the winner, you need to outwork the loser."**

So how do we change this dynamic and embrace this Millennial force? It starts with changing our own perspective first, before we can expect anything else to change.

> "If you want to be the winner, you need to outwork the loser."

Chapter Two

Millennials in the Workplace

"Progress is impossible without change, and those who cannot change their minds cannot change anything."

-George Bernard Shaw

In today's war on talent, organizations struggle to find the skilled personnel they require from only external resources. As a result, many organizations are now required to create programs and strategies to develop talent from within if they want to gain the competitive advantage. Think of succession planning on steroids. Your knowledge workers, the Baby Boomers, are retiring and you must have programs designed to effectively bridge the gap between Baby Boomers and Millennials if you expect to win the war on hiring (and retaining) top Millennial talent.

I had the opportunity to partner with a large Fortune 500 company where the CEO shared, he had just finished hiring a group of twenty-somethings [Millennials]. When I asked him what college they had recruited them from, he said he didn't know, because his firm had stopped hiring American graduates. Instead, they were going to India to find young talent because, unlike Americans, they were ready for the workplace. The American recruits they interviewed he stated, "were self-absorbed, lazy, and unteachable." Ouch!

Please understand, his comments and assumptions do not apply to every college graduate, but it does bring up a critical issue. One of the most crucial challenges we'll face in our lifetime is a global challenge, with consequences right here at home in North America. It will impact everyone. Yet few seem aware of the important dilemma this challenge presents to current and future generations of leaders.

Millennials Do Matter (#MillennialsMatter)

Our greatest generational challenge can be summarized in two statements:

1. The population growth within the Millennial generation is accelerating beyond our ability to attract, manage, or retain them.

2. Older people among the Baby Boomer generation are retiring at the rate of 10,000 per day, faster than we can replace them, and we are running out of time to transfer their industry knowledge to the next generation of Millennial leaders.

Those statements will remain a challenge unless we raise the standard today for those in the younger generational brackets. They can be set up for success by:

- **Mentorship** – invest in them and help them build better social skills.

- **Acceptance** – develop patience and create a healthy balance between life and technology as you work with them and communicate with them better.

- **Leadership** – Lead by example. Help them think and act like authentic leaders or they will continue to struggle with the responsibility they are given in today's workforce.

Extending this kind of effort to our next generation is a critical element in the growth strategy of every organization because Millennials have the potential to become your most valuable employees. They bring a fresh approach to the current ways of doing business. They thrive on collaboration, life-work balance, and multi-tasking. Furthermore, Millennials are comfortable with technology, which can ensure your organization stays up to date on the latest trends.

> Millennials have the potential to become your most valuable employees.

Millennials Dominate the Workforce

The Pew Research Center[1] confirms that Millennials have been the largest demographic in the workforce since 2017, and their dominance will continue to grow. The Deloitte Millennial Survey[2] projects by 2025 that Millennials will make up at least 75% of the U.S. workforce.

Due to this Millennial workforce domination, organizations need to change their recruitment strategies to stay competitive. This includes the way job descriptions are written, where job listings are posted, how interviews are conducted, and how final candidates are chosen.

For those hesitant to step into this new territory of hiring tactics, they will get an up-close and personal look at why Millennials are called the "Job-Hopping Generation," according to Gallup[3]. These facts support the necessary transition organizations need to make to better attract, retain, manage, and motivate Millennials to stay:

- 60% of Millennials are currently open to a different job opportunity (15% higher than non-Millennials)

- 50% of Millennials feel they will not be with their same company next year (10% higher than non-Millennials)

- 36% of Millennials are strategically waiting for specific jobs in other organizations when the job market improves (15% higher than non-Millennials)

As the trends increase, organizations that do not change will get left behind.

A Different Approach is Necessary

There's an adage, that says you can't expect different results by repeating the same actions. This also applies to hiring, retaining, and motivating Millennials. The job descriptions, resume reviews, and interview techniques that have been in place for decades worked for Traditionalists, Baby Boomers, and Generation X, but when dealing with a generation as dynamic and multifaceted as Millennials, those old strategies no longer deliver the same results.

If you need proof, just look at the large turnover rate of Millennials occurring in organizations across the globe. Gallup[3] reports that 21% of Millennials have changed jobs within the past year, which is a rate three times higher than non-Millennials in the workforce. This has cost the U.S. economy $30.5 billion annually, which comes right out of your organization's bottom line.

When the Chickasaw Nation planned to open Oklahoma's largest casino – WinStar World Resort, they saw the trends and wanted to ensure they had a winning hand for their New Year's Eve grand opening. They wanted to avoid the trending high turnover rates, and it was important for them to have a more stable workforce where they could promote from within, when needed.

Since this was outside the norm, it meant they needed to do things differently than they, and other employers, had done in the past. This wasn't easy, because as Lady Luck has taught us, it's a gamble to try something new, especially for a project of this scale.

In order to properly manage and run the different gaming areas, their 395-room hotel, concert center, separate inn, RV park, and 18-hole golf course, they would need 1,900 employees. They also needed each employee to be recruited, screened, hired, and trained within a few short months. Considering the average cost of hiring a new employee is around $4,100, those are high stakes!

Thanks to seeking out our team here at the *Generational Guru*, their gamble paid off! We focused on strategic hiring techniques and training programs for their incoming workforce, which turned into a three-step process: recruiting, retention, and motivation.

Gambling on Different Generations

When presented with all our research about the changing demographics of our nation's workforce and the benefits they would experience organizationally, WinStar agreed with our recommendation to incorporate a multi-generational workforce of their own.

We started by dividing the workforce into the four generations we covered at the beginning of this book: Traditionalists (Born 1922-1944), Baby Boomers (Born 1945-1964), Generation X (Born 1965-1979) and Millennials (Born 1980-1996).

It is important to understand that each of these generations has something special and positive to add to the workplace. Workers in their 60s tend to be reliable, hard-working and dedicated. They can provide much-needed leadership to the younger generations.

Millennials, on the other hand, are ready and willing to work 24/7. They are technologically savvy and love to collaborate. When we bring together all the generations under one roof, the entire organization benefits from its own generational diversity.

At the outset of the hiring blitz, our consulting team determined the average age in each of WinStar's departments. Why? If the average age is too high, the department may be left without much-needed expertise and leadership due to employee transitions.

Generational workforce planning is about balancing the value of a lifetime of experience found in the Traditionalists, Baby Boomers, and Generation X, with the energy and tech-savvy nature of Millennials, with all age groups being an asset throughout the entire organization.

Creating a Magnetic Attraction

As the recruiting process began, we developed an approach that would appeal to candidates in all four generations. First, a **recruitment**

brand was needed for WinStar that would appeal to all generations, as well as consistent brand messaging that would be carried through all communications.

For Millennials, we created a visually appealing, information-packed career website. For more seasoned candidates, we overhauled printed recruiting materials. These included door-hangers distributed in residential areas, which would be sure to reach candidates of all ages. In addition, WinStar ran advertisements in local movie theaters, because all generations go to the movies.

To overcome the distance barrier and reduce potential turnover, we created, designed and implemented a gas program (at the time, gas was around $4 a gallon). Depending on their zip code, each employee would net between $25 and $75 per paycheck, which means we essentially paid the employees to drive to work. And they did! It was a big investment for WinStar, but it made a big impact by keeping turnover down. An additional bonus, it also became part of our recruitment strategy. Another great benefit to this innovative program was that it also improved morale and engagement!

This was a huge task that was completed in less than seven months, and the required workforce was in place and ready to work on opening day. When the doors opened, WinStar was confident it had a winning hand, and that they would find long-term success.

Today's Millennials are Tomorrow's Leaders

Those who embrace Millennials and what they have to offer by adding them to an already generationally diverse workforce will benefit immensely by turning generational differences into a competitive advantage. They bring perspectives that help them better connect with employees and engage with current and prospective customers of all ages.

With few Traditionalists left in the workforce and Baby Boomers retiring, their experience will be sorely missed. Organizations are placing their growth strategies at risk if they solely rely on Generation X to carry the load. Many of them struggle to identify and develop the next generation of leaders, and it needs to be made a greater priority.

Instant Gratification

Going all the way back to Napster, with the ability to easily download and instantly listen to the music of our choice with a simple click, instant gratification has become a big part of everyone's lives, especially Millennials. We no longer must mail a check along with a completed order form and WAIT for our purchase to arrive in the actual mail.

If a Millennial wants to buy something, it's only a few clicks away. They can either download it or place an order and it shows up at their front door, sometimes the SAME DAY! Young adults today (Millennials and Gen Z) have the joy of Amazon, where one-click ordering can have it delivered to their door in as quickly as two hours depending on geographic location.

This is a vital characteristic of a Millennial. **From childhood to adulthood, the world has provided them with whatever they wanted or needed almost instantly.**

As Millennial children, society educated them to expect instant gratification in every aspect of life, for little to no effort, and for little to no exchange of monetary value. For us Gen Xers, if we wanted instant gratification, it didn't happen with a free download or app. Instead, it happened when microwaves gained popularity, and it cost upwards of $800.

Millennials were born into a world where they never had to wait… not even for water to boil, thanks to microwaves and Keurig's.

Just imagine if you never had to share a telephone (sometimes attached to a wall) with a family of five, and instead owned your own smartphone as a growing child that allowed you to call anyone, anywhere, at any time, while checking social media and text! This is the world into which Millennials were born. This generation has always had access to things fast. **They have not experienced some of the struggles and challenges previous generations encountered that were key to building patience, endurance, a work ethic, and the concept of trading value for value.**

When Millennials were in their adolescent years, cell phones were a part of everyday life. Landlines have never served a purpose for them. In previous decades, if you wanted to communicate with someone, you had to catch them via landline while they were either at work or at home. Millennials have never experienced that. They want to talk to somebody now, so they pick up their cell phone, choose their favorite app, text feature, or social media platform, and within seconds they're communicating.

Millennials live on 'quick communication platforms' like texting because "they expect a response now." This has always been their standard way of life and they don't understand the concept of having to wait for things, because never in their lives have, they been forced to wait for anything.

Through no fault of their own, Millennials live with and expect instant gratification in every aspect of their lives.

Many Baby Boomers and Gen Xers do not understand the dynamics that created the persona of Millennials. Because of that, those leaders often get frustrated and withdraw from opportunities to engage and mentor Millennials, yet that is the worst thing they could do! It's time to cultivate leaders within the ranks of your own organization, or it will not survive. It's time to embrace the next generation and understand that a Millennial-rich workforce is truly one of the best ways to position your organization for the future.

Chapter Three

Attracting Top Millennial Talent

"Because the better an organization is at fulfilling its purpose, the more it attracts people who see the organization as an opportunity to advance themselves."

- Robert Shea

It's no secret that diversity helps organizations thrive, and Millennials are the most diverse generation in history. Millennial diversity does not simply mean race and ethnicity, it also includes family backgrounds. More so than previous generations, most Millennials come from single-parent homes, same-sex families, and blended families. Their experiences can help them (and you) substantially in the workplace. When you can effectively attract, manage and engage Millennials you will gain access to their world of diversity and inclusion.

Within the field of learning and development, almost every trade magazine, conference, or blog provides guidance about specialized design approaches and engagement strategies to gain the acceptance of Millennials. In many instances, a hyper-fixation on Millennials has grown within the human capital, diversity, and inclusion fields, affecting just about every facet of talent management: recruitment, engagement, development, diversity, performance management, and succession planning.

When new hires are mismatched with their role, or if expectations aren't properly presented in terms they understand, it could quickly lead to yet another open position in need of a new hire. The long-term costs related to loss of top talent, higher payroll costs, poor customer service, derailed careers, knowledge transfer, and stress-related health issues are enormous. To reemphasize our earlier statistic from Gallup[4], **Millennial turnover costs the U.S. economy an estimated $30.5 billion annually.**

However, there is hope! With the proper education and strategy, Millennials can find their place successfully in multi-generational organizations, but it's going to take a different approach. As Marshall Goldsmith tells us, *"What got you here won't get you there."*

What Do Millennials Want?

What Millennials see as important to their careers might surprise you. Instead of long career paths pursued during the hours of 9 to 5 with the only reward being, a possible pension or gold watch at the end, Millennials demand more – more stability, collaboration, connection, purpose, and flexibility.

They also seek out organizations that support causes they care about so they can feel like they are working toward a greater purpose, one that makes a tangible impact on society.

Here's a closer look at what Millennials want:

Stability

Over 80% of Millennials state company stability is a top priority when considering employers. This doesn't mean they like corporate bureaucracy, but they aren't drawn exclusively to start-ups either.

Furthermore, Millennials grew up in a recession, so understandably, their financial well-being is paramount. This explains why 67% would likely leave their job for higher pay.

Collaboration

Though Millennials are often labeled as "entitled" or "self-serving," 74% prefer to collaborate in small groups. They believe "if the team wins, everyone wins."

Information

Make information about your organizational culture, history, and mission easily accessible, and be sure it is up to date. Millennials want more than a highlight reel of your office holiday party from THREE years ago, they want to know how to land a job with your organization and **WHY** they should go to work for you!

Make social media a resource for job postings, upcoming events, and targeted industry insight.

Sixty-two percent (62%) of Millennials visit an organization's social media sites and Google them to acquire information about jobs BEFORE they decide to even submit a resume.

Connection

During the interview process, allow Millennials to meet other employees, interact with them, and even possibly have a day when they can shadow someone working in a similar position.

Purpose

Sixty percent (60%) of Millennials say they chose to join their current employer in part because of the organization's sense of purpose.

It takes more than money (a salary) to attract Millennials. They need to know they are also making a difference in the world by what they are doing with their current employer.

Personalization

Seventy-eight percent (78%) of Millennials share the overall interview experience is very important to their decision to accept a job offer.

Millennials want to know they're not just a number. Make your recruitment efforts more individualized with personal email communications, social media interactions, and special event invitations geared to attracting them.

Convenience

Because Millennials are fast-paced and more likely to apply from remote locations, video recruiting software gives Millennials the ability to interview anywhere, without involving too much time or money.

Flexibility

Nearly 1 in 5[4] Millennials prefer a more flexible work schedule. This includes a compressed work week with four 10-hour workdays, the ability to telecommute, or a flexible schedule that includes more autonomy and responsibility to get the task done (no micromanagement necessary).

Embracing these preferences can help shape how you communicate and connect with Millennial jobseekers on your career portal and other recruitment channels.

After all, you can't manage Millennials if you can't attract them or motivate them to stay!

Reverse-Engineered Interviews

One of the most effective techniques for attracting top Millennial talent is to have them qualify themselves for the position with your organization and determining if they are a good fit for your organization's culture, vision, and leadership structure. This begins with a dynamically strategic job description. For instance, if you're looking for a Team Leader, enhance your job description title like this: *Dynamic Team Leader*. When done right, the job description will filter out those who are not a good fit, leaving you with better candidates from which to choose, so little time is wasted interviewing people who aren't a good match.

Alyssa Light, creator of the Reverse Engineered Interview, is a consultant who helps companies struggling with high turnover rates to recreate their recruitment process in a way that reliably increases their hiring success.

Since Millennials dominate the workforce, she has become an expert in identifying the right candidates for the job, recruiting them, and then developing incentives and programs motivating them to stay, with a 90% success rate.

She freely shares her biggest tip in her proprietary formula, and that is to have the candidate interview you! Here's how that works. When a good candidate stands out and you are ready to begin the interview process, send them an email with the following instructions regarding the Reverse Engineered Interview.

Dear <APPLICANT>,

Thank you for your application. We have selected you as a candidate and would like to schedule an interview with you on DATE at TIME. The interview will take place at LOCATION (WITH DIRECTIONS TO ROOM/OFFICE IF NECESSARY), you can park LOCATION. Please confirm by responding to this email.

At <YOUR COMPANY NAME> we appreciate the time and effort a person puts into an application and interview. Here, we do things a little differently: You will be interviewing us.
You read that correctly. You will interview us.

It's unlikely that you have a lot of experience leading interviews; we know this. This is about getting to know you as a person. It is very important for an employer to find a good match, and as a potential employee, we understand that is important to you as well. We are not expecting an experienced interviewer in you, we are simply expecting to better understand who you are, and to see if you would be a good fit within our company culture.

<YOUR COMPANY NAME> is a fabulous place to work for people who can embrace this process, who LIKE THIS, DESIRE THIS, and WANT THIS. Conducting interviews in this way gives us the best insight to determine if we're a good match for each other.

1. *Please prepare a list of questions for us and bring them to your interview; no need to send them beforehand. Here are some resources for you to use in preparing for our time together:*

2. *<YOUR WEBSITE and/or BLOG> and/or <SOCIAL MEDIA> Here are a couple of our competitors: <WEBSITES OF TWO COMPETITORS>*

<APPLICANT>, we look forward to meeting you on DATE at TIME.

See you then.

<YOUR NAME>
<YOUR POSITION>
<YOUR CONTACT INFO>

Ps. If we don't hear back from you by <DATE> to confirm your allotted time, we will offer your time to another candidate.

Tips for Success when using the Reverse Engineered Interview

-   People ask questions when they are doing research, are confused, feeling curious, or when they want to clarify something. When a candidate is asking questions, listen to their tone. Watch their facial expressions and body language. If you're not sure what their motivation is, ask a question back.

-   Interviews that are interactive teach us more about the candidate and it teaches them about us. When a candidate chooses you and you choose them, your team has a very strong start.

- Concern or doubt comes out in questions about the past. This could mean something they learned about you during their research and prep, something from their past experiences, or a combination of the two. Confidence to ask these types of questions could be the sign of an honest desire to have a great experience in a new role. That said, it could also mean someone is just digging for information.

- Only you can decide how to answer questions. If you're stuck on an answer we suggest pausing and asking a question back – one whose answer will tell you more about the motives of the candidate. For example: "What makes you ask that question?" asked with a gentle and curious tone (rather than a critical one) is truly a golden question.

Prior to the beginning of your interview process, take time to strategically create three to five standard questions to ask the candidate. You'll ask these after the candidate has conducted their interview with you.

> **The questions you develop should be a representation of your organization's values and culture. Remember, what you ask tells them a lot about you, too!**

The questions you develop should be a representation of your organization's values and culture. Remember, what you ask tells them a lot about you, too!

To help with your assessment of their skills, and to determine if their attitude towards the job at hand is compatible with the job description, here are three sample questions you could ask after the candidate has interviewed you:

Question 1: Have you ever had to wear a uniform, cover up a tattoo, or work at a time that was difficult for you, like early in the morning or late at night? How did you handle that?

The candidate's response will give insight into how they coped with a task that required them to compromise personal style or conform to standards they disagreed with.

Follow up by discussing the most unpleasant aspects of the job, whether it involves grunt work or dealing with rude customers. Someone who still wants the job after hearing the negatives is more likely to last in the position.

Question 2: What do you read or listen to every day to get the news?

The answer to this question reveals the candidate's curiosity and interest in the broader world. Do they read anything beyond Buzzfeed and Twitter?

Question 3: What kind of relationship do you expect to have with your boss?

Millennials may have never had a formal relationship with a boss. This interview question prevents mismatched expectations. Millennials want people to be friendly with them. Working for you may be the first time they have a relationship with an authority figure they don't perceive "as being friendly."

To reach Millennials and achieve better results, your strategies must connect with their habits, desires, passions, and preferences. What has historically worked in the past for peers or older generations is no longer relevant when looking to reach a younger demographic.

Using the techniques and strategies shared here will help you attract Millennials who are a good fit for your team, who are seeking to be mentored and raised up as a future leader who can help bring long-term success for your organization.

Chapter Four

The Millennial Mindset and Work Ethic

"Millennials don't want to be managed, they like to be led, coached and mentored. This generation is on fire and ready to go. Are you ready to change the world?"

– Farshad Asl

Millennials are sociable, optimistic, talented, and a hot commodity for recruiters. What makes Millennials somewhat unique is they are arriving in the workplace with higher expectations and very little experience compared to previous generations.

If an employer does not match and manage the expectations of Millennials, these new recruits are likely to start looking for a new job on their FIRST DAY. This dynamic has a lot to do with how Millennials were raised.

Helicopter Parents

Most Millennials grew up with helicopter parents. Foster Cline and Jim Fay coined this phrase in the early 2000's and it gained popularity as the Millennial generation graduated high school.

It describes parents who would hover over their children – like a helicopter – constantly aware of where their children were at any moment and what they were doing. For example, if a child got a grade less than the parent felt they deserved, parents would typically place blame on the teacher to essentially "save their child." If the child were participating in a sporting event, their parent would hover by making sure their child was treated fairly and didn't get overlooked by the coach.

The children of Helicopter Parents became very dependent on their parents to swoop in and save the day — to be their champions, guardians and protectors. This created a very strong bond between the child and parent, though it made the relationship more like friends than a typical authoritative hierarchy. When Millennials developed this bond with their parent(s), it blurred the line of respect going upward or downward. Parents of this generation are intensely involved in their kids' lives *from the cradle to the workplace.*

While growing up, Millennials were bombarded with consistent and compelling messages. Parenting patterns molded a new generational perspective, an era with its own mood and influences. These messages included things like be smart, be inclusive and tolerant, stay connected 24/7, decide what you want – and go for it.

Millennial parents have instilled in their children the critical importance of education if they want to compete in the twenty-first century workforce. Many Baby Boomers are of the opinion that their own successful career is due in large part to their hard work and long hours. Plus, they still want to offer and contribute so much more to their profession before they retire.

Regardless of a Millennial's education level, their first job might be as a Barista at Starbucks, if they are fortunate. If receptive, they will be exposed to opportunities that will help them learn effective face-to-face communication skills and teamwork in a fast-paced environment!

With most Baby Boomers anticipating longer working futures and Millennials growing in sheer numbers and in higher percentages in the office, the squeeze is on for Gen X, which is the smallest generation, in the workplace. They're also called the "sandwiched generation" since they are sandwiched between aging and sometimes ailing parents, while also still working to finish raising their own children.

Xers find themselves in the tough position of waiting for Baby Boomers to exit the workforce, which provides them the opportunity to create a tighter bond with Millennials. Xers make the best coaches in today's workplace because they understand how Baby Boomers work, and they embrace diversity and technology, which allows them to easily connect with Millennials and what they value.

Millennials are the first digitally native generation, growing up with technology touching virtually every aspect of their lives. Frankly, gadgets seem to grow from their extremities. They developed from toddlers to college graduates with seemingly endless sources of technology-enabled distractions, real or perceived. Over the past fifteen years, teachers have struggled to find the right balance between using computers, tablets, or phones effectively in the classroom and teaching in a more traditional style.

The commoditization of chips, screens, and other technologies has resulted in homes full of computer-aided gadgets, digital services, and technology that operate simultaneously and at increasingly fast speeds. All of this has a tremendous impact on the workplace.

Millennial S.C.E.N.E.

Consider the landscape we now live in. More than any previous generation, Millennials have been defined by technology, which is why I believe it's accurate to call them iMillennials. Why do I feel this is an accurate title? It is because of the intangible impact of the "I" world – the **INTERNET** – on their lives. This generation, born in 1980 and beyond, has literally grown up online. Theirs is a world of iPad, iBook, iPhone, iChat and iTunes; and for many of them, life is pretty much about "I = It's about me!"

Millennials have been raised in a S.C.E.N.E that Baby Boomers have created:

S – SPEED (Slow is BAD)

C – CONVENIENCE (Hard is BAD)

E – ENTERTAINMENT (Boring is BAD)

N – NURTURE (Risk is BAD)

E – ENTITLEMENT (Labor is BAD)

Somehow, adults have created a scenario for young people that looks less like reality and more like a TV show: full of adventure and prizes but ultimately scripted and unreal. Kids today are busy – more than ever – but their activities are about recitals, practice, and rehearsals for games and contests. Their stress comes from a contrived activity instead of a meaningful task. What is at stake is having them value a ribbon or trophy for showing up, instead of doing something of value that takes effort and hard work.

Please don't misunderstand me. I am not saying playing soccer or learning to play the piano is not important. Those activities can help teach children discipline and commitment. However, savvy kids eventually figure out that their activities aren't really changing the world as much as they would have hoped. As an adult, they aren't adequately equipped to handle real stress because they have not had to take real risks that could have negative potential outcomes.

Millennials ask a lot of questions, call out their peers, and frequently challenge authority. This generation is not trying to be disrespectful or rude. They simply grew up in an era where they watched their parents challenge authority (the child's teachers, coaches, etc.). Additionally, they don't need an older, wiser authority figure to get information from because they can quickly answer any question using Google. They are not accustomed to not having the answer at their fingertips because they have been programmed to rely on search engines for the information they need. Millennials are just trying to learn and fully understand concepts.

When their manager, or an authority figure provides them with direction or guidance, Millennials do not immediately accept it as truth. Typically, they will Google it for themselves first. Since they can simply access the internet and find any answer 24/7, this creates the tendency for Millennials to challenge what authority figures say and reject the status quo.

This kind of behavior could make it easy for us to dismiss very talented Millennials or any other generation (who can bring value to your organization) due to being perceived as being disrespectful or seemingly unmotivated. It is imperative we understand their minds because they're simply trying to learn and fully understand new concepts and ways of interacting, not trying to disrespect authority figures or the rules that were put in place decades ago.

In today's technologically advanced world, we must question the way things are being done, as well as constantly challenge the status quo and outdated rules that keep organizations stuck in the past. Otherwise, organizations will not be prepared for the ever-changing needs of their innovatively demanding customers and clients.

Millennials are naturally wired this way, and they are stabbing holes in things that they want to understand more clearly. They don't see any problem with it either. It's not that Millennials are obstinate or unmanageable; it's basically how they learn. As leaders, it's critical you are open to this new approach and leverage the Millennial asset for the future vitality of your organization.

One of the most impressive traits of this generation is that they are automatically looking forward; positive certain things will continually improve. **Millennials have been convinced they can achieve things that have never been achieved.**

Millennials entered adulthood during recession times, right after the real estate crash in the United States. During those years, the entire world was concentrating on trying to rebuild the economy and the media was talking about bright plans for their future. Millennials were too young to care about the economy at the time, but they came of age during the reconstruction years. Due to this, they grew up very optimistic with sunny skies ahead regarding their future. They have always been automatically certain and confident.

The Same, Just Different

It is important for leaders to be aware of, and understand, the different attitudes and expectations of the multi-generational society in which we live, and how to manage it effectively, including the potential collision points that may arise due to work ethic, communication style, and managing change. Best practices such as good communication with flexible leadership styles will increase your opportunity of successfully managing and leading a productive workforce while meeting the expectations and needs of your cross-generational workforce.

> "This optimism [of Millennials] is fantastic and, as leaders, we must tap into it to propel our organizations."
> Sierra Z, age forty-nine, IT Executive

For example, Gen Xers and Millennials share similar needs and expectations, such as a desire for an innovative workplace, flexible schedules, diversity and inclusion, and leaders who walk the talk. Millennials are more interested in hearing that organizations are willing to train them as part of their "role." They aren't motivated by just a "J-O-B."

Consequently, they expect more choices and freedom to pursue their career development. They even require a new type of leadership and coaching style with immediate, ongoing feedback. Armed with the knowledge of this generation's specific needs, developing training opportunities to increase their career growth will enhance their productivity and support your internal retention programs.

The best organizations to work for must be sensitive and embrace the unique needs of each generation and offer what individuals are looking for, such as what makes their work rewarding, which environment is most productive, and what types of workloads, schedules, and policies contribute to a workplace that attracts and retains top talent.

Smart leaders have learned to leverage the diverse backgrounds, experiences and skills of their employees and capitalize on their differences to maximize the organization's ROI.

Experiences Versus Possessions

This leads to another important Millennial trait. Millennials lived during a period fraught with change due to the downturn in the stock market plus the divorce rate was at an unprecedented high. According to the United States Census Bureau in 2010[5], 8.1 per 1,000 population ended in divorce. Millennials also witnessed people losing their homes to foreclosures along with their cars being repossessed, etc. They also watched as their parents who had given their life to their J.O.B. laid-off and lose their retirement savings. With so much tangible and financial loss out of their control, Millennials grew up believing material possessions were of little value. Instead, they value experiences a hundred times more than any type of possession. They value, "What can I learn or do next?" They do not think the same way as Boomers or even Generation X.

For Millennials, experiences create memories, and these are the things that can never be taken away from them by anyone. Baby Boomers were much more inclined to accumulate possessions, believing that success was equal to the number of "things" they acquired.

With the creation of social media, Millennials are observing what their friends are doing across the world. They want to boast about what they did over the weekend, where they had dinner last night, and where they are going on vacation.

Their life values are centered around experiences – not possessions. This is critical for leaders to understand. As you are trying to attract them, retain them, and motivate them in your organization, you need to be mindful this generation is not just motivated by money. They are motivated by the experience they will acquire as part of your organization.

This may be difficult to comprehend because previous generations were more focused on a larger paycheck, stock options, and bigger offices. This generation is unique in that they are more attracted by their next exciting opportunity to grow and learn.

They use these experiences as a measure of status and happiness. Therefore, you will see fewer and fewer Millennials buying homes. They prefer to rent or live at home with their parents much longer to pay off their student debt. This way they can use most of the earnings on what they value. Many of them will also avoid purchasing a car (for those whose parents didn't already purchase one for them). This is because Millennials look at a car as a possession they must maintain, and that cuts into their ability to travel the world and meet new people.

It's important to know Millennials are more motivated by increasing their experiences than increasing their paycheck. This may mean working two jobs and a ton of overtime so they can take three weeks off to backpack across Europe sharing their adventures on social media.

Millennials and Entrepreneurism

Currently being an entrepreneur is a very hot topic for Millennials. Although recent studies show that people under the age of 30 are starting businesses at record low rates, the notion of being an entrepreneur is very enticing for Millennials.

For Millennials there is a big distinction between being an entrepreneur and starting an actual business. For prior generations, these two terms mean the same thing. But during the last decade, the start-up culture has become very sexy to Millennials. They grew up hearing stories about organizations like Facebook, Google and Tesla. Each of these brand-new relatively unknown businesses exploded into a dominating force in their markets.

Millennials quickly noted that being an entrepreneur was the new hot and sexy thing they wanted to do when they grew up.

Media has created a celebrity status around these young successful entrepreneurs. Gen X teens looked up to and followed musicians like Prince. Everyone who was anti-establishment was cool. Now for Millennials the exact opposite is true: the people creating the establishment are the actual celebrities. It is amazing how much has changed with just one generation.

The Work Ethic Controversy

We've established that Millennials want to learn and experience new things. There's a stigma surrounding Millennials regarding their worth ethic, specifically the belief they don't have one. Let's consider some of the reasons why Millennials are perceived as having an undefined work ethic:

1. **School has coddled them.** This may sound cruel, but it is an accurate statement. Sure, they work hard to write a paper or take a test, but it isn't a taste of the real world. For some college majors, students can complete a four-year degree without ever having to attend a morning class. This is poor preparation for the career they hope to have after graduation to help them pay off their enormous student debt/loans. Comet Financial Intelligence6 gives us a snapshot of the true impact of a college education – debt! One in four Americans are riddled with student loans to pay. Upon graduation, the average amount owed is $37,172, which totals out to over $1.53 trillion in total student loan debt.

2. **Parents have protected their children from hard work.** Often, the "real" world is foreign to them. For many Millennials, they never worked during their teen years. They were busy with soccer, piano, and dance classes. This stands in contrast to my teen years, where the average student had to work to make money to buy a pair of Gloria Vanderbilt jeans, (yes, they were very popular in my day). The average adolescent today doesn't have to work until they go off to college or beyond. As their leader, you may be the first person to introduce your newly hired Millennial to a time clock. These extra-curricular activities while important to their growth and development did not effectively transfer into employable skillsets they needed when they entered the workforce.

3. **Expectations have shifted regarding responsibility.** Research reveals that one hundred years ago, four-year-old children were expected to participate in family chores. "Tweens" were working several hours a day and teens were required to be responsible caregivers for their younger siblings. In fact, in one-room schoolhouses, the teacher taught

older students so that they could teach the younger ones.

There is a great sense of idealism, hope, and creativity that Millennials and beyond bring to the workforce. There are important elements sometimes lacking in the skillset of older generations. However, unlike Baby Boomers and Traditionalists, Millennials have been conditioned by a culture of instant gratification, convenience, and leisure. Because our population is flooded with younger generations and their takeover of social media, it seems that society celebrates, and highly values immediately accessible elements that don't require hard work and effort, as previous generations experienced. Sadly, because of this imbalance of perceived values, it reduces the chance of Millennials being equipped to bring a strong work ethic to their first job after graduation.

In the countless survey results I peruse, I continue to hear leaders complain about Millennials, and these are the top concerns:

- They don't want to start at the bottom of the ladder, or even realize there is a LADDER!

- They refuse to understand they have to pay their dues, even if it means they will be better equipped for their next potential role.

- They seem nonchalant about what is required of them to succeed in the workplace.

- They expect a trophy for just showing up to work, never mind getting work done.

Many leaders wrestle with this. If you are leading a group of Millennials, you may ask: "How, do I effectively convey my vision for a strong work ethic to someone who is completely new to the work world?"

Here are a few ideas:

1. **Discuss specific expectations with them upfront.** Have very open and candid conversations about the reality of working conditions and expectations.

2. **Point out their value.** Share with them that while they may be at the beginning of their career, they possess one or more traits that every team requires. If you struggle to come up with genuine traits you can share with them, start with these: they have their youth and eagerly embrace technology. They may have no work experience, but most of them have the ability and interest to participate on teams and committees.

3. **Model what you want.** Take them with you and let them shadow you on projects you expect them to work on later. Show them how you and other team members approach the challenge and task. Then let them know they don't have to emulate your methods because you value their creativity, but you do expect them to model your level of effort and work ethic.

4. **Describe what you want.** Millennials start their first job asking: Where do I fit? What do you value in me? Consequently, it is critical to share exactly what you require from your new hires within the first 24 to 48 hours. Keep it short and concise. Try something like this: **We expect innovation, high-energy, creativity, and a strong commitment to our mission (and**

then make sure they know what your mission is).

My challenge to all generations is to consider the product of someone who's learned the value of hard work (and successfully built a "work ethic"), and then compare that to those who have failed to do so.

The contrast will be telling, and worth much more than any "motivational" speech a leader can muster.

Chapter Five

Transparency, Feedback, and Leadership

"The single biggest problem with communication is the illusion that it has taken place."

— George Bernard Shaw

We know Millennials grew up with 24/7 access to the Internet, and that means they have less perspective on a world where telegraphs, faxes or even cell phones were considered a revolutionary means of communication. Are you having trouble getting in touch with a Millennial? **Use the Internet; they are always connected.**

They are incredibly tech-savvy, can cause a communications breakdown. Be careful about the words you use, verbal or electronic, when communicating with a Millennial. They often have trouble with personal conflict due to their heavy reliance on electronic forms of communication, and the impersonal nature of this medium. The words you use and the way you use them are under constant scrutiny.

Another caveat regarding Millennials: Just because they know how to access all the latest apps, it doesn't mean they know how to understand and utilize all the information they have at their fingertips. For example, when assigned a specific question to answer or topic to research, the first thing Millennials typically do is a Google search. With their fast-paced, multi-tasking, technical agility, they will probably focus on the first answers that pop up in the search, insert that information into their presentation, and call it a day.

However, experience has taught the older generations that just because information pops up on the first page of search results, it doesn't mean it is accurate or from a reliable source. In fact, the first few results that appear on a Google search are paid ads that may not even come close to an "unbiased" report about the topic being researched.

Millennials need to be trained, mentored, and taught proper research techniques, and how to evaluate and use the information they find. It takes time and a triangular approach to find accurate information that can be verified with credible sources and statistics, and it takes wisdom and experience to understand why that is so important in the first place.

There are so many articles out there that quote "facts" that have no verifiable data. Because it's displayed along with an eye-catching infographic it gets quoted and shared again and again.

When I did research our main resource as a student going through primary and secondary education, all we had was the encyclopedia. It was a verifiable, quotable source of knowledge. If the information needed wasn't in it, more research was done on related words and topics through other dictionaries and encyclopedias until enough information was gathered to forge a strong opinion about the topic at hand.

Millennials need to be taught how to conduct their own research and form intelligent opinions based on unbiased facts and statistics instead of parroting what they've seen and heard in their social media feeds and ad-filled Google search results.

The Importance of Transparency

As the Dalai Lama stated, "A lack of transparency results in distrust and a deep sense of insecurity." This is especially true now. Transparency builds trust, loyalty and a strong connection with Millennials. They expect their leaders to be as transparent with them as their parents were.

Transparency builds a level of employee engagement that money, even lots of it, cannot buy. Sharing with people of all ages and levels is vital if you want to keep good people focused, efficient, and productive. The old telephone game has sped up, and today misinformation can travel and snowball faster than at any other time in history.

Organizations today must be prepared to be an open book, so rumors don't get out of control. It is important to communicate when things are going well and when they aren't going as well as expected. Resist the urge to gloss over difficult news by saying things like "Everything is fine, business is doing great" when they aren't, and it isn't.

> "A lack of transparency results in distrust and a deep sense of insecurity."
> Dalai Lama

Millennials want to be in on the truth; they want to know that authority figures in their life and their organization's leadership team respects them enough and trusts them enough to tell them the truth. When people know what is going on, they can use their time productively to help find solutions instead of spending their time gossiping or stirring things up on social media.

Tips

- Assume everyone, especially Millennials, has Google News Alerts sent to them "as it happens" in real-time. It's best if they hear it from you first, before it is shared through the spin of social media.

- Assume Millennials are watching and/or participating in online forums for your industry, and making note of trends, challenges, controversy, and best practices.

- Be aware that your staff, especially Millennials, are following the organizations Facebook and Twitter page and receive notifications when opportunities at your organization pop up on Job Boards they follow!

Communicate what you can — good news, neutral news, and bad news — early and often. Well informed social circles, community groups, families, and organizations tend to have less drama and less gossip, and organizations have less time wasted on employees wondering "what if," which helps build a more trusting relationship with leadership and management.

The Importance of Feedback

Why does this generation need so much feedback?" asks Karen, a fifty-five-year-old office manager. "We hire the best of the best, and I still can't believe how much feedback Millennials need DAILY."

Author, speaker, and coach, Ann Marie Houghtiling shares that "Feedback is a free education to excellence. Seek it with sincerity and receive it with Grace."

Feedback, the need and desire for it, emerges consistently as a theme with and for Millennials. On the one hand, managers groan and complain that they are constantly interrupted with requests for help to ensure they are on the right track, or to see if what they're doing is correct.

On the other hand, although they are quite idealistic, Millennials are also full of great ideas with their "out of the box" thinking, which can only be nurtured with prompt feedback and meaningful interaction.

> "Feedback is a free education to excellence. Seek it with sincerity and receive it with grace."
> Ann Marie Houghtiling

Many leaders expressed the incredulity that their Millennial employees appeared so clueless. "Why don't they know?" was a constant statement in almost every conversation I've had with clients seeking consultations on how to better work with and manage Millennials.

There's a tension that exists between what people ask for and what they really need, leaving leaders stranded between being helpful and being perceived as a micro-manager. The best gift we can give our employees is corrective, respectful, timely feedback in a way that can be heard.

This will help them capitalize on the great things they're doing, and to improve on those skills, saving time and reducing frustration all around. **In the end, feedback is a gift we give ourselves.**

Effective feedback specific to Millennials isn't easy to give or receive, at first. Like all good things, giving, receiving and redirecting feedback into a positive engagement requires us to build that specific muscle so it grows stronger over time.

Timing also counts heavily in feedback. The key is to correct people (give feedback) as close as possible to the moment that it's needed. When weeks or months pass, it can feel like ancient history dredged up to find fault. This is a recipe for disaster in any workplace. Give feedback in a timely manner so your frustration doesn't grow and fester. Tell people how they can improve as soon as you see that they need it, or they may never understand what you expect from them.

Many leaders openly admit they don't want to give timely feedback when an employee is not performing because they don't want to appear mean, rude, or unfair, etc. At what point is it fair to wait six months or a year and then tell them they were not meeting your expectations? This is when you end up in a conflict scenario that is uncomfortable for both of you. At this point you need to clear the air and move forward with much clearer expectations for everyone involved.

Giving feedback that people can understand, absorb, and act on is challenging for everyone. It is so challenging that many managers and leaders avoid giving it, preferring to sidestep what could turn into a conflict situation, or worse yet, a confrontation.

No one wants to keep doing things the wrong way, and if they do, then you don't want them working for you anyway. I believe people want the feedback they need to be effective in their jobs. They want it (and need it) even if it is embarrassing or uncomfortable. They want you to help them do their best. Most of all, they want input and correction delivered in a way that is respectful – a way that honors their effort to date, while offering a better, more effective way to move forward.

Tip

Think of feedback like a bank account. You must put something in (compliments, positive feedback) before you can take something out (constructive feedback). For Millennials to be able to hear you and understand conversations regarding areas of needed improvement, you must first gain their trust through transparency, consistent feedback, and open communication.

The Importance of Access Up the Chain

"I want access to the right person who can help me, no matter what role or position they hold." – Stacey, age twenty-seven, Marketing Assistant

Hierarchy is an obsolete concept for many Millennials. Having grown-up one click away from seemingly all the information in the world, the ability to quickly discern what news is relevant to their life and work and what isn't, all within a few moments, is critical. Millennials

55

see the workplace as a much flatter place than Boomers or Gen Xers did when they were in their twenties. **Millennials don't see structure at all. When they do see structure, it is as a ceiling – not a floor. They see structure as something that gets in the way of their hopes and dreams.**

When asked to rank how important access to senior management is in the job, nine out of ten of the hundred plus twenty to twenty-five-year-old's I talked to or surveyed placed "regular access to leadership" at the top of their list. Doug, a senior leader for a global manufacturing company laughs, "Access to people above me? Oh yeah! My guys go around me and talk to anyone they want to all the time. But they take it to an extreme. They just go and do it without any preparation or thought process."

"On the one hand," explains Doug, "It's good they feel the freedom to talk with anyone in the organization. On the other hand, they don't understand that they could have received a better reaction or response if they had asked to meet with my superior versus just showing up at their office door or stopping them in the break room."

There are a lot of benefits to providing access to senior leaders. It helps senior leaders keep a pulse on what is going on with the new hires and front-line staff of the organization, how the workflow is changing with their Millennial employees' input, and what is on their mind.

A fundamental task of leaders is to promote good feelings in those they lead. Providing direct access from employees to people in leadership positions is the first order of business in achieving this. At the same time, it's not very constructive or efficient for leadership at any level in the organization to spend all their time giving audiences to everyone around them, above or below. Nothing undermines other leaders and managers in an organization more than not reinforcing some sort of structure and reporting authority.

For each organization, in fact, each leader needs a balance regarding access in their culture. What will it look like? What is the standard? What is sustainable? What is the goal of access? Baby Boomers chose to build career ladders and understood they had to work hard to climb the ladder to gain access to the senior leadership team, while Millennials would rather build a lattice framework that allows them to grow and create by learning new skills and having access to leadership and new projects.

Millennials are very confident, energetic, and have wonderful ideas every minute. The challenge for leaders is educating them to know when and to whom they should share them.

Access Requires Feedback

Access without a closed feedback loop is worse than useless. It is demotivating and damaging to the trust you are trying to build with your Millennial team.

If you're in a leadership seat, make sure you give closure or next steps to the different topics that arise during these access times, and be sure to loop in other people in the reporting chain.

Access that Works

An open-door policy alone won't help you achieve your objectives or provide constructive access to Millennials and other employees who want your time. So how can you build a culture of constructive access? Find several avenues for sharing information and getting input. Provide ways to give advice and guidance on critical and non-critical matters that support your direct reports. Share your vision widely.

Practically speaking, what does this look like? Some of it varies, depending on the size of your organization. Effective leadership needs to happen everywhere in the organization, through and with different people. Effective leadership is not silent, and it is not infrequent.

Consider a different matrix of ways to be a present and accessible leader who keeps your people informed, provides access, and walks the line between overly processed and empowered.

Tips

To help with the challenge of access to leadership, here are some ideas:

- **All Hands Meetings**: Hold monthly all hands meetings at which senior leaders provide updates on the organization, have some fun, and shine a light on progress to keep people in touch with management, their personalities, and their vision.

- **Weekly Emails**: If you don't see your whole team weekly, consider adding a mid-week check-in to update your team on the previous activities to let them know about what has moved forward, any staff news, wins, and initiatives in progress.

- **Staff Education and Training**: Share your knowledge, your expertise, and your "special sauce" with your team through interactive training sessions on those topics that support culture (how to give feedback), your organization's mission, and/or skills (presentation, writing, and so on). Develop a video of the session and create a learning channel on your organization intranet that can be shared with new hires. Have the entire team participate over time to broaden the library and share different areas of expertise for the benefit of all.

- **Create a multi-generational committee:** Create a space where matters can be discussed and reviewed in detail by a multi-generational committee. The recommendations can then be organized and brought to the leadership team. This allows for everyone's input and helps build that lattice framework that Millennials desire. Remember to keep the meetings short and concise, as Millennials don't feel like a lot of face-to-face meetings are productive or efficient.

- **Collaborative gatherings**: Have regularly scheduled brainstorming sessions in a casual setting where they can collaborate with one another, designating a leader to guide the group productively and then share the collaborative ideas with the executive team.

- **Feedback sessions**: Prioritize "feedback" sessions, either individually, or as a team. It's not enough for Millennials to just share their ideas. They thrive on feedback about those ideas, so they know where to go next.

- **Appeal to their competitive nature**: Create contests and leaderboards for individuals and teams that have "winning ideas" that are implemented. This will show that leadership listens and values their input.

- **Internal social media tools**: Develop and monitor an internal communications platform that allows employees to communicate with each other directly. You can share the latest employee updates on new hires, promotions, awards, etc. This platform provides Millennials the ability to stay connected to whats going on in real time.

Chapter Six

Lead the Way: Bridging the Gap Between the Generations

"Do not train a child to learn by force or harshness; but direct them to it by what amuses their minds, so that you may be better able to discover with accuracy the peculiar bent of the genius of each."

– Plato

It is important for leaders to be aware of and understand the different attitudes and expectations of the multi-generational workforce and society in which we live, and how to manage it all effectively, including the potential collision points that may arise, such as work ethic and managing change. Best practices such as good communication with flexible leadership styles will increase your opportunity of successfully managing a productive workforce and meet the expectations and needs of your cross-generational workforce.

The best organizations to work for must be sensitive and embrace the unique needs of each generation. They must offer what individuals are looking for, such as what makes their work rewarding, which environment is most productive, and what types of workloads, schedules, and policies contribute to a workplace that attracts and retains top talent.

Millennials, Baby Boomers, and Generation Xer's in management are destined to work together for a very long time to come. **Organizations that effectively assimilate Millennial talent positively and co-create their cultures for the future will have a strategic advantage.**

Leaders need not "bend over backwards" to accommodate anyone of any age to make this happen. However, as leaders, you do need to adjust outdated practices and policies in order to harness the energy and potential of the multi-generational workforce surrounding you. Take time to assess where your people need to adjust their attitudes and behaviors and help them understand how to maximize productivity to achieve your business goals. It can be done!

Leaders don't assume your younger (or any) colleagues know what is expected from them in terms of work ethic, product produced, behavior, dress, or office hours. Remember – Feedback!

- The more you describe what you require, the less chance you have of being disappointed.

- Likewise, when your expectations have not been met, do not wait too long before providing helpful, corrective feedback in a manner that can be received and understood.

> Find time to listen to and talk with your younger team members.

- Building an appreciative culture will improve your team's performance. Find ways to share appreciation for people's efforts and acknowledge good work.

- Find ways to connect with younger colleagues so you have personal insight into how they are feeling and what attitude they take in approaching their work. Read what they read; agree to be a mentor; open your door and find time to listen to and talk with your younger team members.

Smart leaders have learned to leverage the diverse backgrounds, experiences, and skills of their employees and use their differences to maximize the organization's overall mission and goals.

Here are nine tips to use the next time you find yourself needing to Lead, Manage, or Mentor a Millennial:

1. **Create incentives for them**. Share the "WHY" behind assignments and tasks you give them. Remember, young people have a strong filter inside their brains which naturally enables them to multi-task. They process and receive thousands of messages every day via technology.

2. **Micromanage at first.** They are used to accustomed to constant and relevant feedback at home, school, and at work. Most of them grew up with regular praise, trophies and ribbons for simply showing up. Don't be afraid to give them honest feedback. Hold them accountable. Over-communicate. Unlike Generation X who want to be left alone, Millennials want to be watched and noticed.

3. **Let them share their ideas.** They support what they create. Give them ownership by letting them talk. They learn best by being allowed to "upload" their own thoughts, not just receive a download from their boss on what they think they should know. They are accustomed to posting their thoughts

on Facebook, blogs, YouTube, and Twitter. They want to "vote." They want to express themselves.

4. **Launch a mentor initiative**. Millennials want to learn and want feedback, and a mentoring relationship is a great way to incorporate that into your organizational culture. Ask Baby Boomers to share their industry experience and knowledge capital. Ask Millennials to share their technology expertise and social media savvy.

5. **Communicate the importance of work**. They want to know what they are doing really matters. Millennials want to work at a job that has an adopted cause, in addition to simply tending to the bottom line. A cause they take seriously is the state of the environment, so creating "green" initiatives around the office and in your community could go a long way toward keeping them engaged and loyal to your organization.

6. **Tell them the truth; be transparent**. Many Millennials have been lied to by older generations who told them they could DO and BE anything they wanted. You and I know that's not exactly true. We all must align our dreams to our strengths. Not everyone is meant to find their big break on American Idol because they are out of their gifted area, and someone needs to tell them so, gently.

Support your Millennials and help them discover their true strengths and areas of challenge, and then encourage them to play to their strengths and develop their areas of challenge. You may even provide Millennials the opportunity to read StrengthsFinder 2.0, take the free assessment and discover their top five strengths so they can work from a place of strength and not weakness.

7. **Manage by objective**. Be flexible, when possible. Let them find creative ways to use time and resources. They may produce less at home being managed by the clock, than by project. They might do their best work at ten o'clock after they have put their kids to bed. If it's a viable option, try to adapt, and allow them to achieve when they are at their peak every day. Measure their progress by results, not by a time clock!

8. **Mentor NOT Manage.** This is one of the most important techniques. Learn to be a coach. Launch developmental relationships with them by taking them to coffee and getting acquainted with them on a personal level. They love being "in the know" with their leaders and will follow you loyally if you connect with them on a personal level.

9. **Reverse Mentoring.** Pair older, more experienced workers with younger, tech-savvy employees. This helps to motivate both groups to build connections that might not have existed otherwise. Be sure you don't get stuck in the traditional paradigm of older workers passing along wisdom to their juniors. There is a great deal of value in reverse mentoring. Younger workers who may have specific expertise in helping older workers become more comfortable with new ideas, especially with respect to technology

Leadership Styles Across Generations

Organizations that can embrace flexible leadership styles to effectively address the needs and expectations of multiple generations will have a competitive advantage in today's war for top talent.

The following are best practices for each generation:

Traditionalists (Born before 1944):

- Create positive working relationships by gaining trust and respecting their experience without being intimidated by it.

- Gain their confidence by demonstrating compassion and understanding.

- Show them they matter.

Baby Boomers (Born 1945 to 1964):

- Preferred leadership style is collegial and consensual.

- Gain their confidence by asking them if they need support and not just assuming t they do.

- Approach them with respect for their achievements.

- Involve them in participating in the organization's direction and implementation of change initiatives. Let them know they are an important part of the solution.

- Challenge them to contribute as part of a team to solve organizational problems.

Gen Xers (Born 1965 to 1979):

- Respect the experiences that have shaped their beliefs and understanding.

- Tell them the truth, especially when it's hard.

- Honor their sense of life/work balance and need for flexibility.

- Offer mentoring programs.

Millennials (Born 1980 to 1996):

- Respect experiences that have shaped their beliefs and thinking regarding work and life.

- Invite them to be part of a team that exposes them to new areas of the organization.

- Provide them with clear expectations and both short- and long-term goals.

A diversified workforce can help organizations establish a structure that can support and thrive in the ever-changing landscape of the global economy. Every generation has value to offer in bringing up new leaders who will help take your organization successfully into the future as the older generations retire.

Those who fail to tap into the leadership knowledge of those destined to leave the organization within the next ten years will find huge leadership gaps that could greatly limit the organization's overall impact and growth potential over time.

Nine Powerful Tips for Successfully Communicating with and Leading Millennials

Since Millennials currently dominate our workforce, it is important to know how to communicate with them. In any culture, taking time to learn the dialect helps establish mutual respect, common ground, and a deeper relational bond.

The following nine tips will help leaders of all ages communicate successfully with Millennials, and could help gain their respect in the process:

1. Keep it brief, but meaningful

Millennials have mastered the art of saying something meaningful in 140 characters or less. The more concise your message, the more likely they are to relate to it and appreciate what you say.

2. At the same time, provide detail

Just because you're concise doesn't mean you should skimp on the important information. Most Millennials prefer to receive a detailed plan or instruction before jumping into a project. Present everything, they need to know to do the job well, but skip flowery prose.

3. Choose the best medium for communication

Face-to-face meetings and conference calls are not as effective with Millennials. Reach the younger generation where they already spend the most time – on their mobile devices. Try an online team portal for collaboration with a mobile app or get used to Skype.

4.   Understand the 24/7 communication cycle

Nontraditional schedules are becoming more common in business, and Millennials are prepared to work after they leave the office. Schedule digital communication to keep things moving outside of the typical 9-5 work schedule.

5.   Communicate the path to career growth

Clarifying the avenues to career growth is of critical importance to Millennials. A significant number expect promotion within two to three years if they are meeting expectations and performing well. Performance evaluations, feedback and positive communication address this as well as defined career path options within your organization.

6.   Don't condescend or joke about age

Millennials want and expect to be taken seriously at work. Respect them, and they'll respect you. And forget the "This is what I was doing when you were born," jokes, which are tiresome and annoying to everyone, especially Millennials.

7.   Demonstrate fairness in the workplace

Millennials support equality of all kinds. As such, leaders and coworkers must behave in a way that can never be perceived as prejudicial or biased toward or against any individual or group of people. It's not political correctness as much as it is a genuine concern for fairness and equal rights.

8.   Commit to a social bottom line

Charitable giving and corporate volunteerism are very important to Millennials. Make sure you are communicating your organization's contribution to the greater good on a regular basis.

9.   Most important, nurture their passion

This generation more than any other wants to feel as though their lives and what they do, *means* something. Use mission-driven terminology to communicate the overall purpose of your organization, as well as their role in achieving those goals.

Learning the Lingo

Sometimes, it seems like people are speaking in Klingon. With the advent of social media and texting came an entirely new way to communicate. It's a mix of shorthand, conjoined words, abbreviations, and phrases that came about because of a meme or even a mistake on social media that people found funny – and useful – for communicating in a digital age.

Here are a few I've heard or discovered on social media (Thanks, Twitter!) that may help you stay in-the-know:

1.   Phubbing

It means someone is talking to you while he or she is texting or on a computer. It's a negative term only because it's impossible for most of us to talk and type at the same time.

2.   Hundo P

This phrase is somewhat obvious when you think about it. It means "a hundred percent" or that the person using the phrase is supportive and approves.

3.   JOMO (Joy of missing out)

Millennials like to take an overused acronym like FOMO (fear of missing out) and twist it to their will. The "joy of missing out" means missing something that was lame in the first place.

4.   Sorry not sorry

Fake apologies are part of the culture when you are a Millennial. You are a little sorry, but you also want to make fun of the idea of being sincerely apologetic when it is not deserved.

5.   I can't even

When you hear this phrase in the workplace, watch out. It means the person is losing patience, is at a loss for words, and is very upset about something.

6.   The struggle is real

When Millennials use this phrase at work, it means they are annoyed. They might use the phrase to let you know there is a tough problem or a real hardship.

7. On fleek

Used originally in an Instagram post about eyebrows (yes, the origin stories for these terms tend to be as weird as the terms themselves), being "on fleek" means to be on point. In a business context, it means something was well executed and is worthy of acknowledgement.

8. Dipset

I was confused when I heard this one on social media. It means to bail on something — to leave because something is lame. You might "dipset" from a meeting if the topic is boring.

9. V

Another "word" that is a single letter, v is common because it adds some emphasis to texting and social media conversations. It means "very," as in "I'm v excited" about this project. It also means you don't have to type three extra letters.

10. Perf

Another shortened word, perf means "perfect" and denotes agreement to a cause or plan. Like many of the slang words on this list, it came about because you don't have to type as many letters.

11. JK

JK — just kidding — is not a new abbreviation, but it has stood the test of time. It's used when someone has made a joke and wants to make you pick up on the humor.

12. It me

This shortened version of "it's me" is often used as a term of agreement and self-identification. It means the person identifies with the topic, but they don't want to explain at length. It's just a quick way to say you can relate to something.

13. P

Is one letter by itself a word? That's something Oxford will have to decide if it hasn't already, but to Millennials, p is already part of their lingo. It's a replacement for pretty (as in "I'm p excited") and might show up in your next email conversation.

14. TBH

This one is pretty easy to guess (or should I say, "it p easy to guess"?). It means "to be honest" and is usually followed by either a joke or a sincere comment.

This list may help as you see and hear conversational lingo around the office. It's important to know when to use it, and when not to use it, as Millennials are looking to you for proper protocols in the workplace. This, too, is something they need to be taught as you mentor them and help develop them into next-generation leaders.

In the end, it's all about people. No one builds an organization or career alone. We are all in this together. By bridging the gap between the generations and honoring the strengths everyone brings to the table, Millennials and leaders can co-create a future-proof business in which people of all ages flourish.

Conclusion

By 2030, expect a major transformation in the global economy. A realistic projection is that organizations and investors will be constantly responding to changing conditions. Research points to an unprecedented level of volatility in the decades ahead. Beginning in the 2020's transitions will be seen in three major forces impacting the labor force: demographics, automation and inequality. In fact, these forces are already in motion.

Complicated by a world-wide aging workforce, forecasts indicating growth in the U.S. labor force are projected to stagnate and slow to less than one percent per year in the next decade. Loss of experienced top talent in this demographic shift could possibly bring an end to sustained economic growth experienced since the 1970's. With significant improvements in health and longevity in recent years, many people are working well beyond traditional retirement age. However, this trend is not enough to offset the eventual impact of talent outflow and loss of experience in the workforce that has powered the economy in the past.

Consequently, an equivalent or declining labor force will impact economic growth, stalling momentum and creating major challenges for governments. These challenges include: skyrocketing healthcare costs, old-age pensions, high debt levels, housing and homelessness.

Automation has escalated and continues to advance. Partially fueled by a lack of qualified workers, industry and investors alike are turning to technologies to accelerate productivity. The result may be the elimination of up to a quarter of current jobs. Such a reduction in employment will certainly influence the growth of economies, resulting in as many as 40 million displaced workers and stagnant wage growth for many years.

Focusing just on the next decade, automation, demographics, inequality and climate change will add a new dimension to the economic and social pressures already impacting the U.S. and societies around the world. These shifts may create conflict between Millennial workers displaced by technology and Baby Boomers living on Social Security and Medicare.

Truly, remaining current and relevant as a top leader requires continual growth. Evolve, or be left behind. Organizations and leaders must seek help in acquiring the wisdom to develop talent. Those that survive will enhance their ability to understand, identify and embrace change, and the core practices that engage or disengage their employees and customers –of ALL ages.

Are you ready for the Millennial shift? If not, now is the time to prepare.

For more information on how to get the support you need, visit *GenerationalGuru.com.*

What's Next

This book, **Crack the Millennial Code: Strategies to Manage Millennials**, is the second book in a three-part series. The first book in this series discusses strategies that will help you tap into the incredible consumer power of Millennials, and the third book provides you with proven strategies and techniques for motivating them to reach or even exceed their own potential, harnessing their unique skillset.

Be sure to get your copy of the other books in this series by going to **CracktheMillennialCode.com** or **Amazon.com.**

To learn more about developing your own cross-generational workforce or to engage Sherri Elliott-Yeary to speak at your next event connect with Sherri Elliott-Yeary at: **GenerationalGuru.com.**

Notes

1. http://www.pewresearch.org/fact-tank/2018/04/11/millennials-largest-generation-us-labor-force/

2. https://www2.deloitte.com/content/dam/Deloitte/global/Documents/About-Deloitte/gx-dttl-2014-millennial-survey-report.pdf

3. https://www.gallup.com/workplace/236474/millennials-job-hopping-generation.aspx

4. https://www.mastersonstaffing.com/blog/9-interesting-statistics-about-millennials/

5. https://www.census.gov/topics/families/marriage-and-divorce/data/tables.2010.html

6. https://www.cometfi.com/student-loan-debt-statistics

Need Help Marketing to Millennials?

Check out Book 1
Crack the Millennial Code:
Strategies to Market to Millennials

For more information about this book,
to order, and for additional resources, go to
CrackTheMillennialCode.com.

Need Help Motivating Millennials?

Check out Book 3
Crack the Millennial Code:

Strategies to Motivate Millennials
For more information about this book,
to order, and for additional resources, go to
CrackTheMillennialCode.com.

Check out Sherri Elliott-Yeary's
other book:

"CAN Have It All"

Go to *GenerationalGuru.com*
to order yours

Check out Sherri Elliott-Yeary's
other book:

"Ties & Tattoos"

Go to *GenerationalGuru.com*
to order yours

About the Author

Sherri Elliott-Yeary, CEO of Generational Guru, is an award-winning speaker, professional business consultant, and published author who energetically engages international audiences with her practical strategies for attracting, growing, and retaining top talent and loyal customers from every generation. Sherri brings over twenty years of hands-on experience to support you in designing generational solutions that address:

- Cross-Generational Leadership Challenges

- Generational Blind Spots in Sales

- Recruitment & Retention

- Marketing & Communicating with Millennials

- Reverse Mentoring

- Knowledge Capital Transfer

Sherri has provided training and support on generational issues to thousands of leaders and major professional associations across the U.S., U.K., and Canada. Sherri's books, articles, podcasts, training, and consulting explain how generational misunderstandings affect every aspect of a business, including recruitment and retention, management, generational research, motivation, and sales and marketing.

Sherri's unique inter-generational approach integrates the critical elements of communication, sociology, business psychology, and demography to connect workplaces and dramatically improve company performance and sales.

She is passionately committed to helping organizations achieve higher productivity, increased morale, and better retention rates. Sherri offers her clients practical solutions and lessons on improving communication, so they can solve the generational issues that confront their specific industries. She has provided generational insight and advice to the nation's most prominent corporations, including Chevron, Nissan, Pepsi Co., The National Guard, Frito-Lay, Christus Health, Raytheon, Bank of America, GameStop, Citibank, and Marriott International.

Sherri lives in Dallas, Texas, with her husband and sassy dog, Coco. Their three Millennial daughters have successfully launched and are living life on their terms!

You can learn more about Sherri and the programs she offers at . Connect with Sherri on Facebook, Instagram, Twitter, LinkedIn, Pinterest, and YouTube. Her radio show, **Sharing with Sher**, can be found on iHeart Radio, iTunes, Sound Cloud, and Apple Podcasts, etc.

"A mind that is stretched by a new experience can never go back to its old dimensions."

—*Oliver Wendell Holmes, Jr.*